POETRY

The Ground

PROSE

When Blackness Rhymes with Blackness

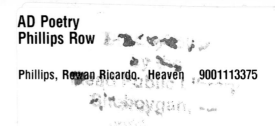

HEAVEN

HEAVEN

ROWAN
RICARDO
PHILLIPS

Farrar Straus Giroux

New York

Farrar, Straus and Giroux

18 West 18th Street, New York 10011

Printed in the United States of America

First edition, 2015

Library of Congress Cataloging-in-Publication Data

Phillips, Rowan Ricardo.

[Poems. Selections]

Heaven : poems / Rowan Ricardo Phillips. — First edition.

pages ; cm

ISBN 978-0-374-16852-0 (hardcover) —

ISBN 978-0-374-71369-0 (ebook)

I. Title.

PS3616.H467 A6 2015

811'.6—dc23

2014039377

Designed by Quemadura

Farrar, Straus and Giroux books may be purchased for educational, business, or promotional use. For information on bulk purchases, please contact the Macmillan Corporate and Premium Sales Department at 1-800-221-7945, extension 5442, or write to specialmarkets@macmillan.com.

www.fsgbooks.com

www.twitter.com/fsgbooks

www.facebook.com/fsgbooks

1 3 5 7 9 10 8 6 4 2

FOR J.G.

Eppure resta che qualcosa è accaduto, forse un niente che è tutto.

The Owl looked up to the stars above,
And sang to a small guitar

EDWARD LEAR

CONTENTS

HEAVEN

THE MIND AFTER

EVERYTHING HAS HAPPENED

Perpetual peace. Perpetual light.
From a distance it all seems graffiti.
Gold on gold. Iridescent, torqued phosphors.
But still graffiti. Someone's smear on space.
A name. A neighborhood. X. X was Here.
X in the House. A two-handed engine
Of aerosols hissing Thou Shalt Not Pass
On fiery ground. A shot-down Aurora
Borealis. That raised areola
At the tip of the tongue of I or Thou.
Benedict Robinson, text me, if you know:
If Hell is a crater to a crater
To a crater to a crater, what then
Is Heaven, aside from its opposite,
Which was glorious, known, and obvious?

—

KINGDOM COME

Not knowing the difference between Heaven
And Paradise, he called them both Heaven.
So when he shrugged at the thought of a god
Blanched in the lights of implausible heights,
Thumbing the armrests of a throne, that was
Heaven. And when he stared out at the sea,
Feeling familiar to himself at last,
He called that Heaven, too. And nothing changed
About either Paradise or Heaven
For it: Paradise retained its earthen
Glamour; and Heaven, because it can't stand
For anything on its own, like the color
Of rice or a bomb, was happy to play
Along, was happy just to be happy
For once, and not an excuse for mayhem.

The soul of swift-soled Achilles, hearing me
Praise his son, silvered, and then was gone,
His long strides causing him to blend, light-bent,
Into the shining, maize-meadow cloudbank
Shadowed by that one solitary tree
It takes sixteen years for light, let alone
A soul, to cross.

                The other dead, who thrived
Though they had died, rejoiced at seeing me
And sang, one by one, to me; and I in
Turn said back to one after the other
That the song that soul sang was a blessing
And that I had never heard anything
Like it; which was true, but also, I must
Admit, they bored me to tears, tears that their
Surprisingly still finite knowledge took
As tears of pure joy from hearing them sing.

Only Ajax Telamoniades
Kept away, arms crossed, refusing to speak,
Dim-starred and disappearing into his rage.
All because of a simple spar of words,

——

A mere speech, and winning Achilles' armor.
Athena above and those men at the ships
Decided that, not me, although it's true
He never stood a chance. By custom he
Should have been given the matchless metal.
How I wish I hadn't won that contest.
How the ground closed over his head for it.
What a fool I can be. Ajax. Who knew
No equal in action but for the one
Man who surpassed him, just-fled Achilles,
So capable of happiness despite
All that happened because he washed up here,
Heaven: this implausible place for us.

Strange that Ajax is also in Heaven
Despite ending his legendary life.
In the end he's won, but he doesn't seem
To understand he's won. Poor Ajax—
As always, I thought I had winning words,
And so I said to him with unreturned gaze:
"Son of great Telamon, mighty Ajax,
War tower, shake free of your anger.
There's no one to blame but Zeus, and look—
He is no longer here, friend. Paradise
Has found you and given you an eternal
Roof under the one tree of High Heaven.

———

Zeus treated us so terribly, and you,
Whom he should have loved like his strongest son,
You worst of all.
                    —But that's history
Now. Come, my strong brother, lord and deserved
Winner of all Achilles wore and was,
Come, be with us here; let me hear the light
Of Heaven in your voice; and let me know,
Because I love you, how you (of all men!)
Ended up in the keen of this endless berm."
But Ajax, gift-eyed, said nothing to me
And took his seat under the rowan tree.

———

LITTLE SONG

Both guitars run trebly. One noodles
Over a groove. The other slushes chords.
Then they switch. It's quite an earnest affair.
They close my eyes. I close their eyes. A horn
Blares its inner air to brass. A girl shakes
Her ass. Some dude does the same. The music's
Gone moot. Who doesn't love it when the bass
Doesn't hide? When you can feel the trumpet peel
Old oil and spit from deep down the empty
Pit of a note or none or few? So don't
Give up on it yet: the scenario.
You know that it's just as tired of you
As you are of it. Still, there's much more to it
Than that. It does not not get you quite wrong.

BOYS

We'd cut school like knives through butter, the three
Of us—Peter, Stephen, and I—to play
Just about all the music we knew,
Which meant that from nine in the morning till
Steve's parents, the ever-patient Murtaughs,
Would get home from work, I played guitar,
Peter played bass, and Steve (who'd end
Up becoming a guitarist by trade
When we went separate ways, to separate
Schools, in separate states), Steve at this point
Played the drums. We dreamed of power trios
And powered our way through song after song,
Including ones Steve and I wrote—like
"Hey, Regina" and the lamentably
Titled "String Her Up." Sometimes we tried out
Some Yes, a long "Hey Joe," the stereo phaser
Was my signature sound, and I'd bend in
And out of notes, imply arpeggios
Only to solo over them, tapped, frowned
Through anything in a major key, felt
My way home on Steve's map of snares, Pete's rope.
We'd play an entire Zeppelin album,

Usually the first or second, then stray
By chance into the longer, later songs
Like bees that float down and drown in a pool.
We'd break for lunch and then get back at it,
As though we had a gig to get ready for,
Or a demo to cut, the cassette deck
Rolling its eyes as it whirred round and round.
Peter, as is the nature of bassists,
Held the tunes together and kept things light.
Years later, I assumed he was dead.
My Telecaster glares at me at night now
From inside the hard case by my bed—
And the calluses on my fingertips
Have long since softened. The six-minute solos
At some point became poems it took two months
Minimum to make seem seamless. Steve
In the meantime thrived in the Triangle,
Became Stevie, married Emily; Pete
I know less about. He posts on Facebook
Cheerfully about the Light, the Great Light
That glows in all of us, sends the occasional
White dove in the occasional shared shot,
A sun resting on a cloud like a pearl
In its mooted gray shell. Nostalgia courts
Me. I'm nearing forty, we were boys—
And I should let us be. But nostalgia

Spreads quickly through the ashes of our youth,
Making ferned fires out of blue beliefs.
When the dark would come, we'd show each other
Our blisters, the painful white whorls peeling,
Our red palms upwards, outstretched and unread.

THE STARRY NIGHT

Night frees its collar from around its neck
And walks slowly past the two bathing bears
Wading in the black stellate subheaven.
They know nothing that's happened or that will.
Their implausibly radiant malaise
Deepening the starry night and its great
Astral ambivalence towards small things
Like bread and Bernardo's first glimpse of the ghost.

THE EMPYREAN

And then the doors drew back and I could see,
Scaling up the high void, plum and pear-green
Parapets, pomegranate balustrades
Portioned by molten silver trim that
Sizzled as it spiraled up and down
The skied poles like boas scoured by lightning.
No structure met them there: they just met air;
Balustrade and parapet, unseen, seen,
Floating where in principle they should be,
As though they were the establishment, and
Not the embellishments. I touched my face
To make sure it, too, was still there. Felt for
It as a frightened fish feels for deeper
Water—. "Who the hell's Heaven is this?"
I asked that half of myself I thought
Might have recognized some familiar thing
Under that star-beleaguered dome, that void,
Where giants moved against the blinding backdrop
So quickly my mind understood them as
Moving slowly as though it were being
Lapped on a track. This was not a Heaven
Of my invention. And that's what scared me:

———

That I didn't make it or dream of it;
I didn't believe in it or buy it.
And yet there it stood: the supreme city;
Feral, spurned, and up on its hind legs
Like a bear before a walker in the woods.

THE BARYCENTER

Alpenglow ripening the mountain peaks
Into rose-pink pyramids steeped in clouds.
How this light, like a choir of silence,
Queues in the air to sing the snowy mass
To shine, I don't know. And yet the chilled dusk,
Remarkable and rude, runs rouge and glows

As though the blue poem of the Earth desired,
And became, the great rose poem of Heaven,
With its champagne peaks and savage thickets
And shrub and break and tangling bushes.
The poem that revolves in two directions
At once, circling us in two directions.

———

MEASURE FOR MEASURE

Alone in Woody Creek, Colorado,
I fell asleep reading *Measure for Measure*,
Right at the part where the Duke delivers
His Old Testament decision of haste
Paying for haste, and leisure answering
Leisure, like quitting like, and (wait for it)
Measure for measure. I saw it performed
Once, in Stratford; I was maybe twenty.
I only remembered the "measure still
For measure" part, until now. It stuck
With me. But the rest of it was wiped clean
From my memory; all of Stratford, too.
Still, the way the actor leaned on that half
Line, "measure *still* for measure," as though it
Were the measure of his self, measure still
For measure, all these years, I remembered
Being the heart of the play, its great gist;
But I forgot it was a death sentence.
Whether Angelo deserved such a fate,
Or Isabella's ability to
Rise above the mire, doesn't matter:

Death, not beauty, woke me.
                              My neck aches.
All of Shakespeare feels like lead on my chest,
Not for death, let's face it, death awaits us,
Usually with less prescient language,
But death measures us with a noun's contempt
For our imagination, being death
But not dying, making do, like when I
Turn from the Bard, look outside, and behold
A herd of a hundred elk, surviving
The snow as they know how—being elk;
An hour ago they were in the hills,
But now they graze a mere five feet away,
Their world othered by these austere windows;
The massive seven-pointer, chin held high
To prevent his thick neck from crashing down,
Hoofs the snow and starts towards me, but then turns
To compass the valley between his horns.

NOTHING OF A BLUE REMAINS

Finally, under thick cover of night,
The snow fell, without wind, and fat as plates.
Wine-rested, I rose a little before five,
Cowed by the darkness of this quiet mountain,
With lion and elk and pheasant roaming
Eight thousand feet above any ocean,
And that much closer to the gates of Heaven
Smuggled somewhere within this small lark's mind
As it sits patiently on a bare branch
Hardly startled when I turned the porch light
On. Something in me, something struggling
Inside me, starts slowly now to feel soothed.
But it's neither from the solitude nor
From the barest blue the black sky became
As dawn turned her silver key in the door.
It will snow here for days. The air is whiter
Than whiteness. Nothing of a blue remains
But for two plump blue jays I'd failed to see
Until the larks began on the final
Tree spotted with snowed juniper berries.
The runts scattered as the two jays
Landed, then three, then four, then six, then eight;

They had been watching the larks all along.
Waiting for them to find what's there to be
Found amid several feet of snow. The tree
Bent but would not give way. And when the jays
Twisted their thankless trunks to pry the dangled
Dark scarlet globes from the tips of their twigs,
They fell, one after the other, like blue
Shards from a shattered stained glass. Then, the larks
Came back and continued as they had been,
Nibbling at what they wanted or needed,
Indifferent to the interruption. Or,
Were they the interruption? These are things
That only the end knows. But the end, like
All I've ever told you, is uncertain.

MIRROR FOR THE MIRROR

This night sky won't always be so Rothko,
Won't always be something you've seen before.
Otherwise, it would always be what it
Was in sheerest separation of is
And as: self separated from self, self
Unparadised, as though there were a place
Somewhere at the end of an endless bridge,
A continent of light, called Paradise.

MONDAY MORNING IN

SNOWMASS, COLORADO

The wintered trees shine white in the white sun
Daydreaming of West Indian dawn—,
Of palms that line the bright back of a beach,
The mazy green hem of a paradise
My parents knew as "home" or "here," conceived
Me there to think their hearth far off
From the Yankee blood in my heart because
Geography is fate and here is mine,
The winter, the nude trees like splintered spears
Souvenired to earth by the fallen
In the promise of *coocoo coocoo coooo*
And, eventually, again, the stirring
Bloom, and the evergreens down the dirt road,
All one, up the mountain path, towards the sun.

—

PARADISO, V: 91–93

And, as the swift-shank sinks into its mark
Before the bowstring has time to calm—
So did we speed into the Second Heaven.

SIN VERGÜENZA

She practices in the mirror before
She has to tell them. But what to wear?
And which tongue to tell them in?

One will curse, scream, run
Upstairs, refuse to come down.
The other will just slowly *tsk*

Shaking his head in shame and silence,
Silence crawling on top of itself
And making more of itself in still more silence.

With disgust saying, "This is sin, you know.
And to shame us like this: ¡la vergüenza!"
Then the mother, who'd run out as though she'd tasted fire

But still wanted to be in the middle of things, booms:
"¡LavergüenzaHijasuciaLavergüenzaLavergüenzaAimíAiai
    AyúdenosVirgen!"
Trapped in two dimensions, naked in the mirror

—

She decided finally to wear white. It's the burden
Of our generations to repeat injury
At times even before injury occurs.

Sin bares las vergüenzas.
And perhaps she will tell them
She loves him

Though she practiced saying to the mirror
That she loves herself
Without shame.

LUCAS AND MARK

I sit sandwiched between two Chuck Closes:
Luckless "Lucas," made up of small fat dots
Bursting against black-backgrounded colors,
His unkempt hair, unkempt beard, unkempt stare
Shot past the small bench between him and "Mark."
No one in the Met has ever looked more eager
To be at the Met than "Mark." Every pore
And razor scrape happens. His bucktoothed grin,
His out-of-focus neck and shoulders share
The running joke of being real with us.
Like Buscemi he is a look of love.
His union-grade plastic frames reflect lights
He alone sees. And now, in twos and threes,
Fans pose with "Mark"'s huge head—the Italian
Girls, bronzed in expensive peasant dresses,
Throw up peace signs and then blow him kisses.
—Meanwhile, "Lucas," left alone to brood
On his side of the room, where he is real
From a distance, instead of the crazed pixels
He's revealed to be up close, drops his eyes
Onto me, as though he knows I'm watching
And hopes I know that he's really a man.

THE BEATITUDES OF MALIBU

I

Walking across the PCH, we looked
Up and saw, big as the butt of a pen,
Jupiter, fat with light and unheighted.
I looked back at the waiting traffic stalled
At the seaside road's salt-rimmed traffic lights
As they swayed to the Pacific's not-quite-
Anapestic song of sea and air—
The raw and sudden crick of crickets—
The cars, suddenly silent as cows—
And blue Malibu blackening like a bee.

II

A poem is a view of the Pacific
And the Pacific, and the Pacific
Taking in its view of the Pacific,
And the Pacific as the Pacific
(Just like that: as though there's no Pacific)
Ends. A poem is the palm of the ocean,
Closing. It or she or he is merely,
Which means it or she or he is a mar.
But a mar made up of temperament and
Tempo—the red weather in the heart.

III

I'm about to get this all wrong, I know:
Santa Monica behind me, the ocean
To my left, Jupiter high above me,
And Malibu somewhere in my mind, flecked
With mist and dusk and Dylan and strange grays
In the sunsets that stripe the seaside hills
Like the tricolor of a country made
Of beauty, the dream of beauty, and smog.
Sadly, in my mind it's always snowing;
Which is beautiful but austere, unlike here.

IV

Along the thin pedestrian passage
Beside the PCH, just off Sunset,
Mel Gibson chants of beginnings and ends
And lies and facts—Jews and blacks being
Both the lies and facts. His face is ruddy
Like bruschetta. He storms at the police
Because fuck them. He's wearing his T-shirt
Like a toga. He schools them his toga
Wisdom from toga times. He offers them
His toga. They offer him a ride—.

———

V

Arun's car carried us like metaphor
In a poem or painting; moving meaning;
Moving the current; being the current;
The terse tug of tides: still the great glamour;
Still, even as we speed on the 110,
The music in my head, the Jupiter
Of the mind's unstemmed Pacific Ocean
As it unfurls in the vapor trail of
Malibu, fragrant in far-off fluorescents,
Like a nocturnal flower calling you.

VI

Then Downtown LA and LA Live surged
Up, like marginalia on a newly
Turned page, spangled with bland suggestions,
Fiery accusations of its own
Brilliance that descend into indifference.
We speed nearer and it grows. We veer and
It grows. We park and it grows. Close your eyes.
Now look. And it has grown. Yo la quiero.
But I should know better, if just because
You can smell the injustice in the air.

VII

The Pacific encircles me. Slowly.
As though it doesn't trust me. Or, better
Said, I only understand it this way:
By feeling like a stranger at its blue
Door. The poet with the sea stuck in his
Enjambments can't call out to some Cathay
As though some Cathay exists and be glad.
No, the differences we have should be felt
And made, through that feeling, an eclipsed lack;
A power to take in what you can't take back.

VIII

The old hocus of this ocean's focus
On pulling its waves over the soft surf
Like a skin pulled down tight over the top
Of a drum was, to her, a new hocus.
We stared out with her, out towards Hokusai's
Tiny boats and rising lace-fringed sea swells
No chunk of haiku could think to charter.
It was like the eighth day of creation
In the eighth line of a poem—she sang,
She didn't sing, the sea sang, then stopped.

———

LIKE SOMEONE WHO SEES

HIMSELF CLOSE TO DEATH

Like someone who sees himself close to death,
Stuck amid quizzed weathers and perilous seas,
And sees a place where he could seem to be
But isn't before his luck's last breath:
This is how I seem, wind-swollen, rank-drawn,
And eyeing in you the cure for it all;
Desperate to pry the dream from the awe,
I'll crisscross the world, chanting this, your song.

(AFTER AUSIÀS MARCH)

NATURE

This is what I sound like when I'm thinking.

APOLLO AND MARSYAS

Go. Go before I change my mind,
Is all He would have thought, and said,
If not for the great glee He heard
In how Marsyas gripped and played
The thin, twig-tied pipes for the Lord
Of Light, Prince of Gods, Apollo,
The Core Verse incarnate, Father
And Avenger of Troilus.
Bonheur blared from the spit-soaked wood
As his left hind leg and hoof stomped
Out one impossible measure
After another as, unsure
Of what we were hearing, we hid
And half-watched, half-blinded by His
Half-presence, from a safe distance.
How happy do you have to be
Before the gods come to stoke and
Then smother it? Poor Marsyas.
Thirty-seven summers ago, when
This bower itself was still young
And on trial, He descended—
Sunluxed, blessed, and blessing with Dawn.

He cooed into the kid's flared ear.
That was all it took, and was. Air.
Air from the Harbinger of Song.
A gift: until he offended
Great Apollo, boasting, "I can play
Almost as well as Great Apollo."
But he couldn't. And he didn't.
And Great Apollo took his prize.
He toyed Marsyas to tinsel,
Then hung his stripped skin from a tree,
And said, I am Apollo: the Power
And Glory and First Song. Burn this bower.
Burn it down——. Then, scribe, write well of me.

THE GOD AND THE GOAT

And then the goat said to the God,
Deliver me my skin. And He
Did. Then the goat said to the God,
Anoint me in my skin again.
—And He did. Then the goat said
To the God, Seal me in my skin.
And He did—. He salved the seams.
And subtled him. And Himself, too.
Call it unrecognizable
Weather: boiling snow sidling
Gilt cloudbanks; a beetle-back sky;
Nacre-gnarled écorchés of ought
And nought air; all caught in the thought
That we were the God and the goat,
Once strangers, now just strange, and bound
By the songs of Heaven and wound
That wing out from our one shared throat.

MUSICA UNIVERSALIS

A planet pulled through a year in the sky,
Like the body of a guitar hauled up
To its headstock, feeling the keys tuning
But far from its sound; the eternal strings,
Gone; the chorus it, even now, still sings: gone.
We are the lost note in the chord of la
Musique éternelle plus grande that was us.

GRAND POÈME PATHÉTIQUE

How long ago was it I jotted down
"Another Nice Poem Written by Rowan"
Before I decided to toss it out?

And what now? What am I supposed to do
Now that I've found it? Ignore it? Pretend
I'd never thought of it? Throw it away?

"Another Nice Poem Written by Rowan"
Didn't give a damn about any of
That or about being nice or Rowan's.

It learned to be fine on its own, without
The tired burdens that being a poem bear.
Another nice poem written by Rowan

Began in a purple-and-light-blue mood.
The sun had set, but the sky was still bright.
It wasn't yet the spring she tasted like.

PARIS PRELUDE

I asked myself, "Well, how did I get here
On the cool shell of this highway-hemmed snail?"
I feel as old as a twin's memory
Of his twin. Et je suis très fatigué.

Even Heaven has its dream of being
Paris. A flawed Paris in a flawed light.
A proper Paris. You arrive there by
Accident: like Narcissus to his pond.

—

TO AN OLD FRIEND IN PARIS

I haven't seen the ghost of your mother.
But I have seen your poems about the ghost
Of your mother as she brushes by you
Near the Seine, or as Linda Gregerson,
Or in the unseen acts guiding those poems
About the ghost of your mother, that chill
As you write that withers into something
Lithe, words for the weather suddenly flush
With lavender and salt, barked line breaks hush,
The poem opening like an ear pressed
Against the cold clicking door of a safe.
Day comes to dark caves but darkness remains.
And the only way then to know a truth
Is to squint in its direction and poke.

NEVER AGAIN WOULD

BIRDS' SONG BE THE SAME

Eight floors below our wide-open window
As early summer sang to early dawn
And no breeze blew, a car crouched idling
Under a red traffic light that had spent
Most of the night with nothing in sight but
The rare bus or cab. I only knew the car
Was there by the boom of its stereo,
That sudden sound stirring me from deep sleep;
Her face facing mine, my face lost in hers,
We'd slept like the lines of a villanelle:
Apart, together, woven into one.
Then I rose and went to the window (how,
For some reason, the mind can't seem to rest
Until it's seen what it's heard and defines
It), and I looked out, and down, but the car
By then had already pulled away, no
Sight of it but for its dragontail of bass.
I still wonder if this really happened:
If it matters in the greater scheme of things;
Is a poem the wonder or the matter?

—

A little later we started our day:
Coffee, the paper, a shower; she asked,
As we Sunday relaxed, if I'd slept well;
She asked me what I was humming; I stopped.
Months passed, then years, and I still have that song
In my head, like a bees' swarm burrowing
Through the skull and finding there my old self,
Which now feels as though it once knew and loved
The city more in that rare heavenly
Moment that it and I were one, just as
"Wu-Tang is here forever" cracked the dawn,
And swerving swallows raptured in Ol' Dirty's
Voice . . . yeah, Ol' Dirty Bastard, aka
Dirt McGirt, aka Ason Unique,
ODB, the Specialist, the dead one.

LIKE A BULLET SHOT

BACKWARDS THROUGH TIME

He prayed his team would win the World Cup.
She prayed he'd just care more. "If that ever
Happens," they both loved to say to themselves,
"It'd be like I'd died and gone to Heaven."

Years later they would meet in Heaven,
Heading in opposite directions. And
Like the last two beads in refused champagne,
They floated past each other and vanished.

—

THE PRIMUM MOBILE

O land of one tree, land of all as O,
Framing all fled feeling with first fire,
As I, the poet Rowan, laureate
Of phoenix nests and ash, never know you.

PAX AMERICANA

In the desert there is a pocket that
Is the poem. A watery bubble on an
Arid surface, like a fingertip on a
Voided screen that sparks to touch. The failed eavesdrop.
It looks like life, or its mimesis, here
Among the droning decadence of dune
After dune, shrugging, as chrysanthemums
Shrug at a burning, chrysanthemum sky.
It looks like life, or its oasis. But
Now at the door, at the edge of enter
Or invade, of live as though no desert
Has ever known you, fathered you, been you,
Prayed for you, to behold the bubble now
From within, the starry dome of pleasure
Above you, the palms' perspiring mists
Made from quietly purring machines, no
Drones overhead, no schoolchildren scream;
Thus the poem, your one true savior, loves you.

———

ON THE END OF THE *ILIAD*

They brandished their births like spears.
Being there wasn't enough. Their names
Needed their fathers and their cities
And their spears and the red air of Ilium.

There's Apisaon lying on his liver
As it curdles and leaks out rib-mangled
From his wound like a clicking tongue
In froth, mind-deep in its porn.

A gray scholar near the end of his talk
Pauses, turns hazel in the maze of his thoughts,
And as he gazes out the window asks,
Why would the father at the end of the *Iliad*

Peer into Achilles' tent and, through the bloodgold fire
And smoke-slow seafog, pismire and simply stare
At his son's stupendous butcher?
He waits for an answer from the weather.

He kneels before the canceling hands of Achilles
That did what they do to the dead of his son
Because they could; and he kisses them.
The father is our first noble disaster.

———

He knows his role. He knows he'll beg.
(Though not for the life: the life's already gristle.)
He'll beg for the body.
He'll beg like a pagan for the body.

Even those who survive Achilles don't.
Priam returned, finally, to Troy's dented doors
And with every step he took
towards the parting gold ruin,

Hollowed-out
Hector
bucked up and
down on his back.

Even iridescent Helen, a trail
Of billowing silks, poured herself
From her paramour's arms
And descended with the rest to see

The sieged city surging to see its broken
Breaker of horses. Half shout: "Hope!"
Half bray: "Brave patriot's sacrifice!"
But Priam can't bear to look at them.

He only looks back dimly at the door.

———

45

NEWS FROM THE MUSE OF NOT GUILTY

He sits in a Hawaiian shirt over a bulletproof vest,
Slumped in a beach chair, its back to the ocean.
Even his red wine spritzer tastes like Skittles now.
It's the same complaint again and again from him: the taste
Of things; he only eats food that he can see made.
And ever since someone suggested he read Sophocles
And put his faith in justice, their talk of having a child
Has been awkward. "That poor, poor child," he says.
"To have to watch out for that poor child," he says.
That poor child. That poor child. That poor child. That poor child.

THE ONCE AND FUTURE KING OF OHIO

Dawn. Two roosters stud the side of the road.
One of them is dead. The other stands there
Stiff in the car's sudden breeze, staring out
Across the hilly Ohio highway,
Skyward towards that something slight of bright
Reds and pinks, a pallid rooster-feathered
Hue, as silent as the rooster standing
And as distant as the rooster on its side.
We drove by, my guide and I, too quickly
To know if one rooster was waiting for
The other, or which had been waiting—,
Or if they'd planned to cross the road together
When suddenly something went terribly wrong,
Either at the end of having crossed it
Or simply, as happens, during the wait.

The whole Ohio highway seemed to know, though,
Like the gate of Heaven you see at death
(As a light or a shining shunning darkness)
Knows Heaven without actually being
Heaven, being rather just a border,
Still part of our plausible world

47

Of parts, living and dead, male and female,
Color and color, belief and belief . . .
There's really no reason to believe or
Not to believe what you see when you see it.
But when at speed I saw those two roosters
Trying to figure out what's next for them
As the distances we traveled on the
661 swallowed them whole with wheat,
I looked from my passenger's seat into
The car's rearview mirror, and saw nothing
That was neither Heaven nor Ohio
As the horses stirred, and the steeples slept,
And the state flattened out like a mirror.
And am I not a mirror for that mirror?

MIRROR FOR THE MIRROR

This night sky won't always have a meaning,
Won't always mean something it's meant before,
For if it did it would always be but
Merest meaning, and how then would I know
Myself from any other self, my self
Beached at the sea of my soul, as it turns
To sing back to this star-seized evening that's
Unreeling and unreals like Paradise?

—

THE MENACE

Call down the world to the world of the world,
Suspend all the harmonies of Heaven.
Listen in the snowfall for the Earth's first
Cooling, for its scent in the chocolate air
As the first snow still falls . . . Is this,
Then, poetry? Always Apollo asked,
Absent of relation to its own mean?
See the world as a problem to be solved.
See the world as a problem to be loved.
Make it again, until you get it right,
So that the first voice sounds like the last voice.

THE DESCENT OF JUPITER
OVER THE MAROON BELLS

When first I looked up
He seemed
An idea in the center
Of a cube of ice, a floater
In the eye of the sky;

But then, with sulfur
On his breath
And thunder in his speaking,
Jupiter descended,
Seated on a golden
Eagle as wide as the sun.

What he said is now lost
To timelessness,
A state no living poet knows
And thus, as my living
Hand writes this, the last
Remaining murmurations
Of his words have been
Sutured by air.

———

He had ended all exile
With a wave
Of his hand

And from the same
Motion twenty
Mountaintops fell:

The careless avalanche
Falling upwards
And quickly corralled
By his glance
Into quintessence of mist.

I bathed in the freedom
Of his rain.

But then I thought,
Without thinking it
Because who knows where
He ends,
About how, in my heart,
Part of me had
Liked being lost
And finding
In the pathways

———

Of the stars
The way to a path and,
If fortunate, to a welcoming door.

Is there a feeling
That can replace this?

For feeling, real feeling,
With all its faulty
Architecture, is
Beyond a god's touch.

Is there a feeling
That can replace it?

Or am I condemned now
By decree,
Like the starving bear
Who climbed the fence
And slaughtered my neighbor's goat,
To be what the god considers free?

———

EXIT TROUBADOUR

The setting sun
Sinks slowly behind
The snowflamed mountain range.

I am not here.
I haven't been
For years.

There's a calm
That explains it as it
Perforates the fields

And then sublimates
For one last time
The mountains' icy shields.

The mist made here
Is all that our
Elegy shall be,

The shunned sun
Still appealing,
Its rind left on the sea.

—

BERNARDO

FOR FIONA AND DUNCAN

Last night of all,
When yond same star that's westward from the pole
Had made his course t'illume that part of heaven
Where now it burns, Marcellus and myself,
The bell then beating one—dreamed some, but
We did not doze. It was a quiet guard.
As quiet as custom. As though silence
Stood watch with us. Then Marcellus started
To tell his tales of brave Norway campaigns.
Again. My hearing palled with the moon's pitch.
And the sickly sky seemed a thing sans all.
I coughed, which I recall because it was
Then that the ghost appeared, though I'd thought him
A mere exhalation, the somber hoarfrost
Of our burning lungs. But it was the ghost,
There in the pendant night, clamb'ring to speak,
But mute, as though trophy of silence.
I called out to it; Marcellus leapt up.
We were like a flame forked by a great wind:
Two waving wildly, made of one matter.

—

And then he departed. We thought it best
Not to dwell on the thing, our ghosted glimpse,
Which could have been but time's spark and love's fire
Caught in both of our eyes somehow. What say
You, Marcellus? Or have I said it all?
O Horatio, Horatio, had
You only been there. Poor Francisco, sick
Of heart he has been: I imagine you
Have heard, perhaps from himself (so Spanish
With his feelings). But you, Horatio,
Had you been here! I yet can see the stage,
And your brave "Stay! Speak, speak! I charge thee speak!"
And wager would I my post that that ghost
(Were it that) would have stayed and given you speech.

AN EXCUSE FOR MAYHEM

The Kingdom of Heaven, the Kingdom of
God, Kingdom of the Father, the Kingdom
Of Christ, House of the Father, the City
Of God, the Heavenly Jerusalem,
The Holy Place, Paradise of Life, Life
Everlasting, the Joy of the Lord, Crown
Of Life, Crown of Justice, Crown of Glory,
Incorruptible Crown, the Great Reward,
The Inheritance of Christ, Eternal
Inheritance, the Immutable Change,
The Belt of Venus, the sublime blue hour
Of the voice, the mute light, mute church, mute choice.

VALL DE NÚRIA

The white rose. The celestial silence.
The lake of light. The bed-like inner thigh
Of empyrean buttermilk and gold,
Call it what you will, it wakes me tonight.
Heaven reheavens. And the mind's prelude
To the touch of your lips on my forehead,
On my neck, our drowned echoes celloing
In the dark like flames drawn on the ocean,
Is not the mind's prelude but its heaven.
How somewhere not in Spain there's a mountain
Borrowing your name, my soul is its snow,
And so in the summer I am nothing,
When all I want to do is lay my head
Down, lay my head down on the naked slope
Of your chest and listen there for my heart.

ACKNOWLEDGMENTS

Many thanks to the editors of the following publications, where these poems, or versions of them, first appeared: *Aspen Sojourner*, *The Buenos Aires Review*, *Callaloo*, *Harvard Review*, *Granta*, *Grey Magazine*, *Likestarlings*, *Literary Imagination*, *The Literary Review*, *Little Star*, *The New Republic*, *The New Yorker*, *The Paris Review*, *Poetry*, *Tongue: A Journal of Writing & Art*, and *TSR: The Southampton Review*.

"*The Odyssey*, Book 11, Lines 538–556" appeared in Poem-a-Day via the website of the Academy of American Poets.

And a special thank-you to the Aspen Institute, the Aspen Writers' Foundation, the Catto Charitable Foundation, and Daniel and Isa Catto Shaw for their grand hospitality.